NO AUDITIONS
FOR
THIS ROLE

For Dana

Joy and Peace

Sondra Childers

NO AUDITIONS
FOR
THIS ROLE

REFLECTIONS OF **A PASTOR'S WIFE** AND HER FRIENDS

SONDRA CHILDERS

Pleasant Word
A Division of WinePress Group

Unless otherwise noted, all Scriptures are taken from the *New King James Version,* © 1979, 1980, 1982 by Thomas Nelson, Inc., Publishers. Used by permission.

Scripture references marked RSV are taken from the *Revised Standard Version* of the Bible, copyright 1952 [2nd edition, 1971] by the Division of Christian Education of the National Council of the Churches of Christ in the United States of America. Used by permission. All rights reserved.

ISBN 13: 978-1-4141-0801-8
ISBN 10: 1-4141-0801-X
Library of Congress Catalog Card Number: 2008912059

This book is dedicated to Howard, who invited me to share this life with him, and to Sam, Ben, and Jake, who joined us and provided such joy in the journey, with my deepest love and gratitude.

CONTENTS

ACKNOWLEDGMENTS

MANY PEOPLE HAVE encouraged me in the writing of this book. Early on I sent incomplete manuscripts to our sons, Sam, Ben, and Jake, and daughters-in-law Christy and Courtney. One son responded, "Wow!" Good friends Denny and Joy Walker and Dale and Kathy Bruner also read early manuscripts. They gave positive responses, encouraged me to keep writing, made good suggestions, and even said they would buy the book if it got published. My special long-time friends Carla Kupp and Jane Scott read early copies. They responded, "What a treat!" and "I loved it." I am very grateful to them. Such encouraging words, as well as my own deep desire to write for and about pastors' wives, kept me going in this endeavor.

I initially sent out an invitation to several pastors' wives I know, asking them to contribute from their own stories, if they cared to. Included in the book are writings by Jan Butterworth, Nina Clark, Sharon Craft, Darlene Gronhovd, Kim Holmes, Susan Parsons, Jennifer Roberson, and Sue Shoop. They were candid and honest in what they wrote. I learned from them and often identified with their words.

My daughter-in-law Christy contributed her touching perspective from growing up as a "preacher's kid," and our son Jake gave me a personal look at a situation that occurred for him when we went back to visit churches where his dad was pastor.

My husband, Howard, has always been supportive of this project, offering his own ideas and memories and giving me the okay to share experiences from his roles in both seminary and his different pastorates. What fun it has been to laugh with him over our past experiences and foibles! It has also been humbling. I continue to be grateful for the life in ministry that we have shared.

I must especially thank my friend Ann Shults, who got me started writing and kept reminding me that these stories needed to be written. She had heard some of them in small group settings from time to time. Ann shared her home in the country as a place for me to start writing and provided instructive books for the process. She is one of the best listeners I have ever known.

To the team members at Winepress Publishing who were in charge of my book project, I owe so very much gratitude. My Project Manager, Christine St. Jacques, was wonderful in her help and encouragement. I was blessed to have her in that role. The re-writer and the copy editor gave such helpful comments and suggestions.

They, too, encouraged me in this project. For the book cover, I had only sketchy ideas in my mind, but I shared them with the designers. I was thrilled with their design.

Most importantly I give thanks and praise to God. I firmly believe that He gave me this project and was with me throughout the process. I am so grateful that He allowed me to participate in life as a pastor's wife. There was no audition for that role, only His grace all the way.

PREFACE

"I'VE ALWAYS WANTED to be a minister's wife!" I heard that comment years ago from the wife of a recent seminary graduate who was being interviewed for a position on our church staff. I was not mistaken—those were stars in her eyes as she shared her enthusiasm with committee members sitting around the room.

Not too many years later, after her husband had become a senior pastor in another church, this same young wife sat in our living room, sharing once again. This time though, the stars had morphed into tears. What had changed? Had reality overshadowed her idealism?

As a pastor's wife, I have long felt the desire to help other women in the same circumstances. I've invited some friends to add their stories to mine. For some time now I have kept a list of subjects pertaining to being a pastor's wife. My list started with humor, and I wondered why. Then I remembered our very first pastorate. I wish I could tell all the not-funny-then, but oh-so-funny-now stories we lived through there. I think I will try. But I'm getting ahead of myself. It is my deepest hope that what I share in these pages will be a little entertaining and a lot of help to cheer, bless, and encourage pastors' wives.

INTRODUCTION

TO THE BEST of my memory, I never held a personal conversation before the age of twenty with a minister. I certainly never thought I would one day marry one.

During the summer between my sophomore and junior years of college, I was working for my dad in his architecture office. One afternoon, I came home from work, and my mother met me at the door announcing, "There's someone here to see you."

I went into the living room and found a gorgeous hunk of manhood in an army uniform. I had never seen him before, though he later told me we had met a few years earlier at my sister's wedding. *And I didn't notice him?* Hmmm, I wonder where my head was that day?

My mother had followed me into the room and finished her introductions by saying, "He's going to be a minister."

"That's nice," I replied. Period. Five minutes later he was gone, and two things happened. My mother burst out, "I want that young man for a son-in-law," and my sister chimed in, "He's dating someone else."

Regardless of that "someone else," he called the next day, and we went out for coffee. After that, we dated steadily. Sometimes our dates were traveling surveys around the Texas Panhandle as Howard went door to door in small towns asking the locals what they thought about having a Presbyterian church in their town. On Sunday mornings, we drove to the little town of Happy, Texas, where he preached and led worship.

After six weeks of almost daily phone calls and many dates, he asked me to marry him. And I said "yes." During that time, he tried to explain what my life married to him could be like if he became a "circuit rider in the Colorado Rocky Mountains" (his words, I promise).

One night when we were on a date, he suddenly stopped the car and said, "Let's pray." My heart pounded, my palms became sweaty, my breath shallow. I had never prayed aloud with another person, other than the blessings before a meal. I have no idea what I prayed, but at least the ground was broken for the next step in our relationship. Howard continued to surprise me in different settings by asking me to pray or ask the blessing. It was like he was leading me to take baby steps in my Christian growth.

My life changed forever after that day in our living room. I had grown up in the church, going alone if necessary, and I attended Sunday school until college and continued to attend church while away at school. My own faith was simple, my Bible reading sketchy. Jesus was a revered name in our family. My sisters often sang Christian music, both at home and in public. However, I had never "given Him my heart" in a personal way. I had never even heard that phrase used.

In 1958, Jesus came into my heart as I opened the door for Him. One of my sisters paved the way for that when I was very young. I have three older sisters, and one of them spent a lot of quality time with me. She taught me how to swim, but the most important thing she did sounds a little incredible, even now. When I was seven years old and she was sixteen, we sometimes went on long walks together in our town. When we reached our destination, usually a cow pasture full of Hereford cattle, we sat and ate a picnic lunch. As we did this, she would read to me (remember, I was seven years old) from Thomas à Kempis's *The Imitation of Christ*. When I graduated from high school, she gave me the very book she had read from for a graduation gift. I still have it. It is a wonderful treasure. So is she, I might add.

Howard and I waited to marry until after his first year of seminary, thinking long engagements were important. That's probably true in most cases, except that we were sixteen hundred miles apart. That was a hard way to get acquainted, much less conduct a courtship. During that time, many people offered me their advice on what I needed to be, do, and become in order to be a pastor's wife. Few told me I already had qualities that would serve me well in that role. I could not have listed any, since I had never thought of myself as a pastor's wife.

My only desire was to marry Howard, and God seemed to be giving both of us the go-ahead.

Howard came home in June, and we married three weeks later. Two weeks after our honeymoon, we were leaders at a church camp for junior high students. Howard was the speaker, and I was a counselor to a cabin of girls. I don't remember that I had a chance to "test the waters" in my new role as a pastor's wife. It just began to happen, continued to grow, and never stopped for the next thirty-nine years.

CHAPTER 1

NEW MARRIAGE,
NEW PASTORATE,
NEW LIFE

AT THE END of his first year in Princeton Seminary, Howard was called as student pastor by a little country church. The church was twenty-five miles from campus in a lovely little town of four hundred people, most of them related in one way or another. I had no college degree, but the three-room elementary school hired me to be the kindergarten teacher. As far as I know, the only reason they hired me was because the Superintendent of Schools was a member of that church.

In September of 1959 we left Texas and headed for New Jersey in our VW Bug, which was loaded down with our few possessions, including a large Adler typewriter so I could type his seminary papers, sermons, and the church bulletins.

Standing in the manse driveway when we pulled in, a woman greeted us with the words, "I hope you don't

1

have a dog." (I guess I was expecting, "Welcome! We're glad you're here.")

At that time, we didn't have a dog, but guess what our first purchase was? Dottie Beagle was a bargain pup, because her tail had been broken. It looked like a flag on the end of a pole. Buying her was most likely our first mistake, and a big one. It never occurred to us that we were hearing a plea from the church ladies, who had been cleaning up dog hair in the manse prior to our arrival. (Our predecessor had a Collie.)

Dottie was really cute and became a great companion for us, but she was a disaster where that church was concerned. Disaster #1 came on the day when all the church members showed up with food items for our pantry. In former times this was called a *pounding*, and it was meant to be a positive experience.

Everyone came shortly after church let out. Pretty soon, two ladies approached me and asked if they could see the upstairs. A rather odd request, I thought, but I dutifully led them up the stairs. As we reached the landing, I looked back and saw that *everyone* wanted to see the upstairs. Nothing had prepared me for this experience or for what was about to happen.

First stop, our bedroom, where one of the women walked directly over to a wall to straighten a picture hanging there. Then I led them down the hall, where they had to dodge the ironing board I had used before church.

Howard's study was at the end of the hall. It was furnished with a desk, probably a bookcase or some one-by-six boards stacked on bricks, an over-stuffed chair, and a hassock (footstool). The church ladies had decorated this room also. However, while we were at church and our puppy, Dottie, was free to roam the house, she had decided to re-decorate Howard's study.

As we all peered around the corner through the doorway, there was a dead silence. Dottie had torn up the hassock, and the stuffing was all over the floor. She had also found and chewed up the red pencils Howard used. Strange as it seems now, I don't remember *anyone* saying *anything*. I guess shock does that to you. We all just turned around and went back downstairs. But I knew, oh boy, I *knew* that somewhere in the chronicles of the Stockton Presbyterian Church, there would be a giant black mark beside my name. I've never understood why they wanted to see the upstairs—maybe to check out my housekeeping skills? They already knew all the furnishings, because they had provided them.

Disaster #2 did not involve Dottie. It so happened that the lady deacon, the same woman who greeted us in the driveway, was also our next-door neighbor. Her husband was a big, burly railroad engineer who loved gardening. One Saturday, when Howard was in his study, I decided to rake the ankle-deep pile of leaves in our front yard. I piled them in the driveway that we shared with these neighbors and went in to ask Howard what I should do with them. Distracted, he said, "Put gasoline on them and burn them." What he should have said was, "Put a *drop* of gasoline on them and burn them."

It is a miracle that I am even here to tell you that I soaked about a fifteen-foot stretch of piled leaves in gasoline and then lit a match. Howard thought someone

3

had fired the Civil War cannon in the neighbor's yard across the street (it was pointed directly at his study window). I unexpectedly found myself flying backwards across our yard, sans eyebrows, and—horrors!—our neighbor's hedge was on fire. Black Mark #2.

I guess you could say that we went on to spend the next three years alienating a lovely—if a bit odd—congregation of God's people. One day Howard and I played softball in our back yard and broke a church window (thankfully, not a stained-glass one). Dottie, bless her, ate the hat that one of our members left on our bed after church one day. When Dottie got loose, she loved to ransack the neighbor's flower garden, looking for rabbits.

It does not take much imagination to figure out the consternation we caused that congregation in that otherwise peaceful little town. Truthfully, those were our nursery school, pre-school, and kindergarten years in the pastorate.

Howard worked hard applying his seminary training to his work as a student pastor. One summer he called on one hundred homes in and around our community, inviting the residents to our church. One of these was the home of Robert Goulet's "Camelot" understudy. He and his beautiful wife had been visiting our little church. When Howard knocked on the door, this man looked out the window and then said in his beautiful, booming voice, "Oh hell, Honey. It's the minister." We swallowed our pride and visited them anyway. All the church really wanted was someone to preach every Sunday whose wife would teach Sunday School, help lead the youth group, attend all the women's meetings, type, print, and fold the Sunday bulletins, sing in the choir...and maybe not burn down a member's hedge in the process.

On Saturday nights, Howard and I went over to the church to mimeograph and fold the Sunday bulletins. We took Dottie with us, and she roamed up and down each pew, eating the chewing gum off the bottom of the seats—her way of serving. She pulled the ultimate caper just a couple of weeks before Howard graduated from seminary. He had neck surgery around then and was laid up in bed. One Sunday a friend and fellow student came to preach for Howard. My mother-in-law lived with us then, and when we left for church that morning, we apparently didn't shut the front door completely.

We were quietly listening to our guest's sermon, when out of the corner of my eye I saw a broken white tail zip down the center aisle of the church. Then up front on the chancel next to the pulpit stood Dottie. No one moved. (They were counting the black marks.) When I came to my senses, I ran to the front, reached down to pick up my dog (who by then had squatted on the carpet), only to have her go limp and fall off the chancel, yelping loudly. Meanwhile, no one in the congregation had yet to move or utter a sound, much less come to my aid. Finally, I managed to scoop up my dog and slink out of the church...forever.

5

Well, not quite forever. Thirty-four years later, we paid a visit to that little church. After the service was over, one of the women approached me and said, matter-of-factly, "I still remember that beagle you had." What God taught me and I suppose serves as a moral to this episode in our lives was, "Don't buy a beagle."

So what did we buy for our second dog? A beagle. Actually, Howard and I did learn a valuable lesson from his first pastorate, but it took us a while to realize what it was: love the people, accept them where they are and not where *we* want them to be, be willing to move along with them and beside them, and grow in the Lord together. Neither arrogance nor a "doormat" mindset is a helpful or desired characteristic for the Lord's servants, whether they be ordained leaders, persons in the pews, or pastor's wives.

As it turned out, the Childers were not the only providers of "entertainment" in Stockton. The town had a volunteer fire department, and its members were scattered among the town's churches every Sunday morning. Some creative guy came up with a plan to "free" all the volunteers during the sermon once in awhile. The siren would go off and two or three guys would leave the pews to go for a drill. My husband eventually figured out that the "drill" was actually a "kegger" down on the Delaware River bank.

A night came when all these well-trained volunteer firemen had to answer the call to an actual fire. A small, historic building called the Creamery was burning. The whole town gathered around the site to see the volunteers save the building. Thermoses of coffee and cocoa were passed among the crowd. As it turned out, the Creamery burned to the ground, because no one could figure out how to attach the hose to the water source.

We got a second chance for more coffee and cocoa late one night when a drunk driver hit the only fireplug in town. That was no small feat, because it was located about fifteen feet from the edge of the road. Water spewed everywhere as all the townsfolk appeared in their bathrobes to watch the excitement. The manse was strategically located for all these events, so we were always in attendance.

CHAPTER 2

MOVING ON

HOWARD GRADUATED IN 1962, and we moved to Texas on faith, without a pastorate, church staff position, or a home to move into. There was at least one reason that things turned out this way. During his last year of seminary, Howard had a chance to be interviewed by a pastor from the Seattle area, a great man. Howard wanted very much to work on his staff.

When the time came for the interview, Howard was still recovering from short-term amnesia brought on by a serious fall on the ice that winter. The interview took place on the seminary campus very early in the morning. The pastor would ask a question, and Howard's temporary loss of memory would kick in. So, in short, the interview went poorly.

Just a few months later, however, Howard's seminary buddies who were members of this pastor's church went to bat for him, knowing how badly Howard wanted to be on his staff. They persuaded him to give Howard one more chance, and he agreed to do that. This time, we were to meet the pastor at a restaurant in Greenwich Village in New York City. I have no idea how this particular setting was selected.

The pastor had only a short time, as he was due to meet someone else to attend a Broadway show. On a Friday night, we arrived with another seminary couple and took our seats at the tiniest of tables in the most crowded, loudest bistro in the area. We sat elbow to elbow, not just with our tablemates but also with folks at the other tables inches away. Dr. Munger shouted questions across the two-foot span.

It went something like this:

Dr. Munger to Howard: "What is your *vision* for Boeing?"

Howard to Dr. Munger: "What's Boeing?"

In addition, my co-workers had been teasing me all day about keeping my mouth shut, so the interview would go well. They were teasing, but my subconscious was fried, apparently. By the time we arrived in New York, I had the most stupendous headache of my life. I could not see or think, much less speak coherently.

In minutes it became evident that the men did not share the same vision for the associate pastor position. Dr. Munger's goal was to evangelize Boeing Aircraft's thousands of employees, and Howard had no idea about that.

So we headed for Dallas after Howard's seminary graduation. The Presbytery members in the Dallas area promised that they would take care of us, and they did. We spent the summer living with Howard's aunt in her one-bedroom apartment, so Howard, Dottie Beagle, and I slept in the pull-down bed in the living room for a couple of months.

Howard and I traveled around the state during this time as he did some guest preaching in various churches to provide a measure of income. His name had been put in to become the pastor of a new church development congregation in the Dallas area when it opened up in the fall. Before Howard was called to this pastorate, he did an interim for one month in a small town in East Texas. It was there that I got a questionable word of advice from an elder's wife.

While we were putting a meal together in her kitchen, she told me it was important for the pastor's wife to be the *first* one to laugh whenever he said something funny from the pulpit. I did not take that advice to heart.

In September we moved into the manse, and Howard began his ministry with the new church development congregation in the South Oak Cliff area of Dallas. It was the 60s, and lots of turmoil over desegregation was evident in Dallas schools and neighborhoods. Those were the days of the not-yet united USA and US Presbyterian denominations. A US church (the southern Presbyterians) about a mile away from us was older and seemed to be flourishing, while our little congregation struggled to grow. Our members were a blue-collar group of dedicated folks, plus a handful of doctors in residency at the nearby VA Hospital, who would be moving on before long.

This time the manse was not furnished. When we left seminary, we owned two over-stuffed chairs, a couple of antique pieces, and a coffee table. Our salary was to be $5,000 a year, so Howard's aunt introduced us to a kind banker who helped us by giving us small, short-term loans whenever we found a piece of furniture we needed.

The manse had a thirty-five-foot-long den with a green vinyl covering halfway up the wall and a linoleum floor. Services were held there before the church building was finished. It was so hard to furnish that room! We even resorted to going to a pickle factory and buying a pickle barrel for $5.00 to use as a lamp table. The only thing we had in our dining room the first year was our Christmas tree.

I still typed Howard's sermons and the church bulletins, which he printed on those inky mimeograph machines. We had the added tasks of mowing the church lawn as well as our own and preparing monthly reports to get out in triplicate to show the details of Howard's work to Presbytery, Synod, and General Assembly, from whom the church had loans. Since we were in a larger community, I found more outside interests to enrich my life. I was a nurse's aide in a hospital, became a member of a Fine Arts Society, played some tennis, and joyfully became a mother for the first time when we adopted our nine-day-old son.

At church I was active in the Women's Association, and I specifically remember going with members of that group to a presbyterial meeting in another town. We rode with Edith, who hydroplaned at eighty miles per hour all the way in a driving rainstorm, talking the whole time. I made a mental note not to do that again. For entertainment, Howard and I found a small lake outside of town where we could go bass fishing for two dollars. Of course, Dottie was always with us. We did not use a creel, but simply tossed the bass up on the bank. Imagine our surprise when we could not locate them later. No, they didn't slither back into the water. Dottie had buried them.

One morning, after we had lived there a year and a half, we woke up to see one hundred fifty "For Sale" signs in our neighborhood. We were told that the School Board had come up with a plan to get around desegregation laws. Whenever a neighborhood school had a majority of African-American students, that school was declared to be a school for African-American children. Oddly, it became a sort of a leapfrog atmosphere, as many white folks then moved on to the next all-white neighborhood rather than live in an integrated neighborhood. In our neighborhood, the church of another denomination across the street from us moved with them (for the third time). We stayed and fended off the opportunistic real estate brokers and American Nazi Party with their scare tactics. We got to know and enjoy our new neighbors. Howard and the Session explored ways to minister to our changing neighborhood. They met with the session and pastor of a nearby African-American church, and made plans to unite the two congregations under a co-pastorate. That would also result in uniting the two denominations, because the African-American church was US.

The USA Presbytery voted in favor of the merger and was planning to pay two-thirds to three-fourths of the money to fund this ministry. So it was with glad anticipation that Howard and I, along with the other pastor and his wife, attended the US Presbytery meeting in East Texas. But it was not to be. There, after leading us to believe it was a "done deal," the Presbytery voted it down. We had a very sad, quiet ride back to Dallas that day. Adding to the disappointment and embarrassment was the fact that the US African-American pastor had a PhD *and* a ThD and was the president of a nearby college.

Howard was eventually called to a young church in Colorado. The pastor who followed him in Dallas, a seminary classmate, was a good fit, and he and his wife kept the church going with innovative ways for that unique ministry. To my knowledge, there are no white folks living in the lovely Singing Hills neighborhood of Dallas today.

I tell this episode from our ministry to show what a contrast it was to our student pastorate in New Jersey and to emphasize that it was the Lord, who is always the same, who sustained us in each setting. I can't imagine how the first two churches we served could have been more different.

While we were in Dallas, a more experienced pastor's wife gave me some valuable advice. I was still confused about my role within the congregation. The expectations members held about my position and my own concept of what it involved sometimes put me in an overwhelming situation. This more experienced pastor's wife told me,

"I just tell them I'm an Indian, not a chief." That one comment helped me put my role into perspective.

This searching for role understanding was not unique with me. Another pastor's wife whose husband was in seminary with mine wrote, "I had no background on what it would be like to be a minister's wife. During seminary, it seems to me most of us wives were trying to figure out what our roles would be when we were in our first calls." She went on to say, "I was really scared that I would be expected to teach and do all kinds of things that I wasn't sure I *could* do."

I decided to put that good word from the older pastor's wife into practice in the Colorado church shortly after we arrived. I turned down a request to be an officer in the Women's Association. My desire was to keep a peaceful retreat at home for Howard and raise my two little boys (we had adopted our second son after the move to Colorado, when he was seventeen days old.). I did that for the next six-and-a-half years, but not without criticism. In those years, I always taught Sunday school and vacation Bible school, took part in small groups and The Mariners for young couples, and held gatherings of all kinds in the manse.

Yet my refusal to be an officer did not sit well with the involved women of that congregation. I do believe their motives were good when they asked me. That particular arm of church congregations has never proven to be in my comfort zone. However, I did faithfully spend the seventeen years of our last pastorate as an active member of the Women's Association and a Circle. I was greatly blessed by those women.

CHAPTER 3

NEW DISCOVERIES AND GROWTH IN EXPERIENCE

MY EXPERIENCES AS a pastor's wife seemed to develop in me a no-win syndrome. Although this may not be true for every pastor's wife, some comments shared with me recently lead me to the conclusion that this may be common. One friend wrote, "Maybe that's what being a pastor's wife does to most of us…just beats us down so we believe we are pretty worthless. It's what I've fought the most since being here." This was from one of the most gifted Christian women I know. I dearly love her, so this grieves me. Venturing to make a generality here, I would say it is possible that many pastors' wives have felt that way at some point.

A contrasting view came from a pastor's wife who wrote me with candor:

I do have a lot of good and some bad. But I finally decided on this: I had made up my strong-willed mind that I was going to fight this Minister's Wife stereotype as hard as I could! For the most part I did. I was supportive of [her husband] and was involved in the church as much as I wanted to be. But the surprising thing was the way the church met me. It was like these wonderful people had themselves written I Corinthians 13. They were kind, not puffed up, always loving, believed in both of us even when I think we were a little squirrelly. I was received into a community that became my family. I feel like they raised me and showed me I only had to be myself. They were always there with their love, something that I could have never anticipated. That congregation gave us something that every minister's family should experience, and I feel so blessed that I had it for twelve wonderful years. It was a real gift.

Was her experience unique? I don't know. I believe that her report is much more than seeing the glass "half full." It is, rather, a testimony of a pliable heart that God worked with to show her how love looked among His people. It sure sounds like that congregation's loving personality was already in place when my friend and her husband arrived. How fortunate for them. They are an easy couple to love, I might add.

Another wife shared from her experience:

"I married my very best friend the spring of 1968. By that time, I had come to terms with the Presbyterian Ministry thing, somewhat. Thankfully, I had grown to know and love two dear women who were pastors' wives, and they shared some very valuable insights with me about the 'role' I was inheriting. I would not be the person I am today, had it not been for those two women. I would have tried very hard to please all those members of all those congregations and be the 'Pastor's Wife' that they expected of me and not able to express who I really was. I simply could not play the role, so I chose to be just me, and not ask for a 'script' from each congregation that we were a part of. And it worked!"

From what she has shared, it looks like it is a matter of choice for a pastor's wife to be herself and not take on *expected* roles and titles. It is not necessarily an easy thing to do for every pastor's wife. Not all of us have enough confidence in ourselves and/or knowledge of who we are to automatically know our place in a congregation and be comfortable with it. It's those congregations that are able to accept us without laying any stereotype on us that help us find our way.

One wife found her way through the small group movement so popular in the 1960s and '70s, and the women's movement that started about the same time. In small groups, Christian people learned (in her words) "to take off their facades and be honest about both the good and the bad in their lives." Through the women's movement, she learned that she had her own gifts and did not have to be "someone else's appendage." In discovering her gifts, she became less dependent on her husband and became a small group leader and a Sunday school teacher. She worked outside the home and eventually went back to college to get her master's degree in pastoral counseling. In all of this she had gotten much support from her husband and family.

Sadly, she writes, "This was when one of the women in the church decided to take me aside and let me know that she was very disappointed that I had made these decisions, because the young women's group was obviously more important and in jeopardy without my involvement." Fortunately, in her husband's next pastorate as she continued work in the master's program, she never felt judged by those in the church. When she began working in a mental health program and became executive director, she felt the whole church was proud of her.

A good friend, whose husband was on staff with my husband at one time, has written that they have also been in churches where the people have allowed her to be who she is. Being a pretty social person and getting her energy from being with people, she was comfortable with the church activities, retreats, holiday dinners, and the congregational meetings. If she had a struggle, it involved having too many identities...as in being "Ron's wife," "our pastor's wife," or her children's mom. "Who am I really?" she sometimes wondered.

She and her husband were grateful for the help the church gave in raising their children. I was intrigued with her statement that "all it took was teaching them (their children) basic manners." They were taught always to be polite and respectful to everyone in the church. Sometimes she and her husband had to work out "trade-offs" with one child or another over what activities they would be part of in the church. There was no forcing or pressure to be part of something that created a hard time for them. Their individual personalities were considered and respected. Wise parents in the manse, I'd say.

I recently asked our sons and our daughter-in-law to contribute from their experiences of growing up in a minister's home. Our daughter-in-law wrote that she remembered a time when she was in college, and her dad asked her if he and her mom did anything that encouraged the faith that she now had as an adult. Her first thought was that we parents (she included us here!) somehow made it fun. That comment has a good ring to it. She went on to say, "Faith in our lives didn't mean that we had to be serious all the time. I knew faith was of great importance…I loved going to church. It was initially a social thing for me, for sure, to be honest, but it got me there!"

Some challenges for her were the issue of her dad not being home much in the evenings, something she remembers her mom talking about when the children were little. Another thing was being conscious of peoples' perception of her because of what her dad did. She was afraid to tell people his profession because of the conclusions they might draw about her. This next statement really touched me and hit home. "I also had to fight the perception (from others) that my dad only worked one day a week. It really bothered me that people thought this, because I didn't see anyone else's dad working harder."

Amen.

One of our sons has shared about how hard it has been for him to return for visits to congregations his dad has served. At those times, several people would come up to talk with him, and he couldn't always remember their names. This was an embarrassment for him, because *they* usually called *him* by name. I understand this dilemma. How grateful I was in one congregation for the sweet woman who always said her name to me when she greeted me in our early days there. What a contrast she was to another woman in the same church who chirped (with a twinkle in her eye, I think), "I bet you can't remember my name!" Twinkle or not, it was still stressful, because I really did want to remember her name.

I found that each church where my husband served was unique in its expectations and requirements. It reminded me of how I always thought that all I had learned and used to raise my first child would naturally work with the second one. Wrong! Different personalities, you see. Church congregations are much like that. In one church, the pastor's wife was not expected to have a high profile. I once gave a children's sermon in that church, and one woman commented afterward: "It's a sad day when *the minister's wife* has to give the children's sermon!" It wasn't that I was not qualified. More likely it was that I had a stereotypical title attached to my name, and I was not considered as simply one of the members of the congregation.

In another church, a young woman told me that it was okay to be Howard's wife, but "just don't get in the way of his ministry!" I would try to unpack that comment, but it's painful to think about. I have always wondered what she would have defined as "getting in the way" and if I would have agreed with her. These encounters felt a little like I was caught in a rundown between first and second base. Either way they were going to "get" me. Interestingly enough, pastors' wives can be criticized for doing "too much" or for doing "too little." Although not always the easiest, the best plan is to be yourself and slough off any criticism, perceived or real.

After Howard retired, the church we attended in Colorado had three pastors whose wives all had high profiles. I watched in amazement as each one was allowed to use her gifts in many different areas that benefited herself, her husband, and the whole congregation.

The senior pastor's wife in that church shared her *next-church* experience: "Maybe that's what being a pastor's wife does to us…just beats us down until we feel we are pretty worthless. It's what I've dealt with the most since being here."

See what I mean about churches having different personalities?

Truthfully, I have never needed or wanted a high profile, but I did want to be useful. Where I was drawn in comfortably in one congregation, I might be pushed away in that area in another one. In each new congregation I had to find my way into the fold. Some pastors' wives have obvious talents that can be put to use immediately—like singing in the choir or playing the organ or piano. That did not apply to me. One thing I enjoyed very much was leading small groups and Bible studies. Teaching Sunday school was another area I liked and was able to do in each church we served. Over the years, I think I pretty well covered all the age groups in that area.

Pastors' wives cannot be lumped into one stereotype. We're all different, even though we share many similar experiences. Our backgrounds, personalities, self-image, education, talents, health, outlook on life, faith—all these vary.

I have known many pastors' wives in the past fifty years, and I have discovered suffering in most of them. One of my favorite seminary wives took her own life just a few years into their pastorate. Another pastor's wife suffered from chronic colitis. Still another had *two* nervous breakdowns. When her husband retired, he was honored and remembered for his work at a Presbytery meeting while she was never mentioned. Yet this woman raised three sons who all became ministers! Is that not a noteworthy feat? A word of thanks could have made all the difference for her.

CHAPTER 4

NITTY-GRITTY ISSUES

WHEN HOWARD AND I were first engaged, the wife of my sister's pastor pulled me aside one day to give me her word for my future, based solely on her own experiences. "You cannot wear bright colors. You will not have any friends," she said. And there she stood in her olive drab dress and no make-up, modeling her very words. At that time I was a real greenhorn, but even so, I refused to believe her. I didn't allow her words to sink in very deeply. The fact that *she* believed it made her quite lonely and isolated, I'm sure, and that makes me sad. Also, she was not a member of any sect that had a dress code. She was a member of a mainline denomination, and how she came up with this notion remains a mystery to me. That's one requirement that no one ever laid upon me, at least not to my face.

Not quite so drastic, these following issues are ever-present:

- high expectations (from the congregation, your spouse, family members, or even yourself)
- loneliness
- low self-image
- resentment

High Expectations

Although we are in a new age in the church, high expectations occur in every congregation in one way or another. These include:

- constant attendance at worship
- endless potlucks
- involvement in women's meetings
- impeccable housekeeping
- the highest personal grooming
- a positive and pleasant demeanor
- perpetual hospitality
- superb listening skills
- boundless compassion
- a supportive attitude toward her husband
- unfailing control of her children

I'm not making this up. I have been pulled aside on one occasion, by a woman in our church who wanted to "fill me in" on the lack of housekeeping skills of an associate pastor's wife.

I would have loved being all these things to everyone all the time, but Super Woman I just wasn't. I tried to be a good listener while holding a hungry infant or tracking down a youngster who was racing around the church halls, ignoring the glares from church matriarchs or the parents of "well-behaved" children. Stressful? You bet! Conducive to attentive listening? Maybe not. The natural order of activities for any normal church family? Of course.

What I love about pastors' wives, though, is that they carry on, and they do care about others, whether they are criticized or not. If one is in command of her own emotions at these times, maybe she can get out of some uncomfortable situations with a little humor. Maybe.

One wife told of her ambivalence about the expectations of others versus what she wanted to be in the role of minister's wife. She went to a conference where the leader made the point that minister's wives have a lot more power in their roles than they realize, and that it can (and should) be used in positive ways. The implication here is that we wives can hinder or help what our husbands are trying to do in leading the congregation. The conference leader she mentioned used the words "make or break," which are a bit too strong for me. I don't believe I've ever heard of a pastor being asked to leave or getting in trouble, because his wife was wreaking havoc in the church. Then again . . .

Loneliness

Loneliness is a reality for *senior* pastors' wives. Our first year in one church, a Valentine's banquet was held for young married couples. It was well attended and had an air of romance in the decorations and program. Part of the program included one couple renewing their vows up front with my husband leading this ceremony. All the other couples stood holding hands and facing each other, also repeating their vows to one another. Guess who remained standing off by herself, trying to blend in with the wallpaper?

What gets me now is that whenever these kinds of things happened to me, I always felt guilty that I couldn't handle them better. Perhaps Howard was aware of my dilemma, but he could not "fix" it, because of his leadership role. It took me a while to get over that lonely, embarrassing night. As I look back now, I ask myself how important that event was in God's plan for my life. Sometimes perspective changes with the passage of time, and issues dim in importance. Thankfully.

One friend has written that she is lonelier in their current church than she has been in two others her husband served. She attributes it to this being her husband's first senior pastorate. In her words, "the difference between being an associate pastor and a senior pastor is extreme!" Not as many "warm fuzzies" floating around, and the load her husband bears is heavier and sometimes unpleasant.

If I may use a metaphor here, it's not a matter of caring for the "forest" only—the expectation is that each individual tree must be cared for and nurtured and tended to. What if the church has 1,300 members? Or even 80? One pastor with 80 people bringing their issues of health, divorce, unruly or "lost" children, anger at their denomination, expectations for how the church should be run, misunderstanding of God's love for them, adultery, loneliness, pride, alienation from friends or family, material needs, loss of job—things common to all congregations—equals exhaustion and many headaches for a pastor.

Maybe the pastor's own family has some of these issues, so he meets them when he walks through the door of his house. Whether this is the case or not, when he leaves the church, all that "baggage" may come home with him. Why? Because he cares, and he knows God cares, and it's his calling. Enter the understanding wife who comes on the scene to listen and hopefully lighten some of those burdens, knowing he cannot share many of them with her. It takes a thoughtful and caring wife to lay aside her own burdens of the day in order to give her husband a little retreat time when he comes home from the church. Unfortunately, it doesn't always happen that way. I know. I'm a flawed pastor's wife.

A recent letter from a pastor's wife in another state resonated with loneliness. Recovering from the scars of a previous traumatic church experience, she tried to adjust to the new parish but found herself incredibly lonely. She writes, "I minister to my husband so that he can serve the church, and he gives back to me what he can, but we do not get any support from church members. My problem is: who cares for the pastor's wife?"

She also spoke of what it's like when she attends church in their present parish. She has noticed that the only people who talk to her are her husband, the staff, and her children. No church members call to offer help when her husband is out of town, and she is left alone to care for their three young children. So she questions, "What is wrong with me?" I counter-question, "What is wrong with those people?" What she misses most is community and authentic friendships, something everyone wants and needs. She comments, "Everyone is friendly with me, 'the pastor's wife,' but no one is my friend."

I believe her experience is a contagion among many churches.

When I recently shared this wife's comment with another pastor's wife, her eyes filled with tears. She is in a similar situation in their parish. Other wives have shared their frustrating search for friends among the congregation. One wrote, "…although we took part in group activities at the church, we had few friends we did things with as couples. I don't know why it is still true for some of us that we are treated differently in that way. Do the people think we don't want friends to do things with just as couples?"

One pastor's wife wrote and told of her recent experience of loneliness and how God led her out of that. She had a vision for an outreach ministry for her church and needed others to be in on it. She invited a small group of women to a meal in her home and shared her vision with them. They caught the vision that day, so the group began to meet together regularly and pray and plan how to carry it out.

After a little painting and decorating in the church basement, the group held their first outreach event. It was a luncheon for their staff and the staffs of a nearby church and a shelter down the block. Thirty-five people attended, got acquainted, and shared their lives with one another. Another event was planned to honor the music team. God gave her the women and the gifts of each one to work with her and carry out a new ministry. She is no longer lonely, and I can hear her joy in what she shared with me.

Resentment

Resentment is an unwelcome attitude, but sometimes it happens. In my life any resentment was probably connected to what our family had to give up because of the church calendar.

One of a pastor's wife's most important tasks is helping her children somehow understand (even when she may not understand herself) that their dad's current project at the church must take priority over family activities or plans or desires. It's also true that many of our family activities took place within the church, our larger family. That was OK, except that Dad was usually preoccupied and engaged in relating to the members, not his own family. Then it was my job to keep the children from tugging on their dad's pant leg, while he was talking with "Mrs. Bigelow" about her upcoming surgery.

This was often hard on my husband. Given a choice, he would have sometimes chosen time with us instead. The ministry is a far cry from 9 to 5 every day. I think 24/7 would be more accurate.

Low self-image

One thing I've learned after many years: Go to the Lord. Go to the Lord. Go to the Lord! I am sorry to say, too often that was the last place I thought to go. It took me such a long time to fully understand what He could do with failures and doubts, hurt feelings, and mistakes. I kept looking around for my "advocate," but I was looking for one in human form. My really, truly, never-fail Advocate was always within me and right beside me. He's still there. He's very patient.

Nevertheless, I had periods of depression (which ran in my family anyway). When the depression got debilitating, I sought counseling. Sometimes counseling improved my outlook and sometimes it didn't, but I've never regretted going for help. I know other pastors' wives who have had counseling. It's not something to be ashamed of. Ever! The shame would come from suffering with depression and not seeking help.

However, with some Christians, talking with a counselor comes with a stigma. They take it as a lack of faith. I beg to differ. God uses physicians and counselors for our growth and healing. I remember one man who had a problem with my going for counseling. He was in our home visiting my husband and asked where I was. When Howard told him I was at a counseling session, this man shot back, "But she has you!"

Of course, Howard helped me with some issues in my life, but our emotional closeness automatically made some of my problems beyond his reach. I needed a person trained in counseling who could interact with me objectively.

CHAPTER 5

GRACE IN THE TIME OF NEED

ABOUT THIRTY YEARS after I became a minister's wife, I attended a women's retreat in south Texas, where I wrote "Sondra's Song." The words came to me one afternoon, and I quickly put them in writing. At this point, I finally realized that more than my going to the Lord, it is He who comes to me:

In acknowledging your greatness, O my God, I feel so small. So I take your hand in trust and love and walk into our future. For You and I– we travel together, and I'm not going without You! Today You lifted me up when I remembered your love. How encouraging! For my failures and feelings of inadequacy seem to loom before me like great flashing neon signs. I am weary, full of self-doubt, and sometimes even despair. The well of energy and creativity, even activity, is dry. Yet, mercy and love, power, grace, and patience are what I experience of You. Please accept my gratitude and be my hope.

> I love You.
> Your daughter in Christ,
> Sondra

A cherished event that occurred about this same time was a trip I took to a healing conference in Colorado. After one session, the leader gave an invitation: anyone who wished to have a time of prayer could stay. I sat down with a woman and a young man and began by saying: "I have been a pastor's wife for thirty years, and I am very tired!" The first words out of the woman's mouth were: "*Thank you* for the thirty years."

Tears of release flowed immediately. I was not expecting those words, and they helped me so very much. I believe they came straight from the Lord. I walked away from that experience with a much lighter heart.

During this same time, my husband was having his own case of burnout. It looked something like this:

1 burned-out pastor
+ 1 burned-out pastor's wife
= numbness, "deafness," and generalized fatigue

There was nothing more to give. The cupboard was bare. The well was dry. Thankfully, it was not a fatal condition. We took off a few extra weeks in the summer to renew our energy and recommitment to the work. Fall brought a new sense of purpose, energy, and joy that year.

I could name several pastors this very moment who are desperately in need of a full sabbatical or at least a long respite from their pastoral duties. My husband and I are praying for them and their spouses and children. A pastor fulfills many roles, and a major one is as caregiver. Caregivers wear out. Caregivers need care. Some might say, "Well, that is why he has a wife!" I'm not going to carry that load of guilt, because pastors' wives are also caregivers. They, too, wear out and need care.

In 2001, after Howard had retired, we attended a seminary reunion. While there I heard in a sermon a wonderful quote by W. H. Auden. I love it! It goes like this:

"He is the Way.
Follow Him through the Land of Unlikeness;
You will see rare beasts, and have unique adventures.
He is the Truth.
Seek Him in the Kingdom of Anxiety;
You will come to a great city that has expected your
    return for years.
He is the Life.
Love Him in the World of the Flesh;
And at your marriage all its occasions shall dance
    for joy."

Ah, the "land of unlikeness"—something I've always believed about being in the ministry and serving congregations. No other profession, calling, or work contains all the aspects of life in the ministry. Some similarities exist, but there is no perfect match, not one. Can you imagine saying to the plumber, "I think your

35

wife should come with you and stand at the bathroom door while you fix the faucet!" Or to a lawyer, "When is your wife going to have an open house for your clients?" Or to a doctor, "I think your wife should teach the Lamaze class!"

"Unique adventures"—I'll always be grateful for them: witnessing the baptism of a young Jewish woman in a neighborhood pool in Los Angeles; or going to the Yakima River to watch my husband baptize several young people, while the congregation gathered on the bank; sitting outdoors in the interior of Zaire in 1990, at the table of a Zairian Presbyterian elder and his family, as they, along with the American missionary, sang a hymn to us in their own dialect; visiting Mr. Joe Durham in his one-room shack located on the Trinity River bank, and hearing him say that if he lived anywhere else, he would not be able to tithe.

"Land of anxiety"—of all the days of the week, only on Sundays do I rush to the restroom several times more often than usual. That physical reaction sure smacks of something big going on in my spirit and psyche. I was surprised to find that the problem did not go away after retirement, either. A friend once reminded me that I had said at one time that I was a *private* person in a very public role. That probably explains the physical phenomenon.

So, I "love him in the world of my flesh," and that is enough…for now. There have already been dances for joy too numerous to count, I suppose.

CHAPTER 6

THE JOYS OF CHILDREN AND VACATIONS

SPEAKING OF JOY, I want to introduce our sons. We raised three of them, both in manses and in homes that we purchased with housing allowances. They are my heroes. My journaling included all that they personally contributed to their dad's ministry in various churches. Although often used as an epithet, PKs have a special place in heaven. I'm sure of it.

The following is a list of our sons' service for the Lord in the churches where their dad was pastor:

They faithfully attended Sunday school, VBS, and youth groups all during their growing-up years. They helped lead worship in special services, gave children's messages, worked at church camps and Young Life camps, held Young Life meetings in their homes, got up before school to attend YL Campaigners Bible studies, went on mission trips—one to Alaska, one to Mexico, one to Brazil—where a home was built, a pastor's manse was worked on, and a surgical ward was built for a medical mission hospital. They were Sunday sextons, getting up early to open up the church and turn on lights and heat; had singing parts in VBS programs and children's Christmas pageants; wrote Advent devotionals for the church Advent book; attended membership classes; taught Sunday school; delivered Thanksgiving baskets...the list goes on.

They are resilient and forgiving and hardworking. We still learn from them. How we love them!

If there were such a thing as family merit badges, each of our three sons would have one for camping. That was our style of vacationing for many years, and I have marvelous memories from those times. When our sons were growing up, we camped in a large cabin tent in Big Sur; Glacier National Park; Lake Louise, Canada; Yellowstone; and locations in northern New Mexico and Colorado.

On the mornings we were going to break camp, we would pull the boys, still in their sleeping bags, out of the tent, and while they slept on, we folded up the tent. One year, the two older boys brought two friends, who were also brothers, for a camping trip in Yellowstone around the middle of June. Also along on the trip were our youngest son, just three years old, and our Chesapeake Bay retriever, Sandy. One day they had a great time splashing in the nearby stream. That evening the clothesline rope sagged under the weight of five pairs of wet jeans. The next morning, we awoke to a five-inch snowfall— and jeans that were flat, frozen slabs!

One year in Glacier National Park, a ranger took our toddler son with him to bait a bear trap, possibly a trap for the bear that had visited Howard in our campsite earlier that morning. The next summer, the same ranger, his wife and three children arrived at our home in Colorado. Part of our hospitality was finding a "home" for his horses while they stayed with us, so we lined up a good friend who had acreage at the edge of town.

As the ranger drove around the circular drive at our friend's house, his truck caught the edge of our friend's roof and ripped it right off the house. That turned out to be one of those "all's well that ends well" times, though. The insurance paid for repairs, we had a good visit with the ranger and his family, and our friendship with the homeowner continued.

Although we may have chosen camping because it was the most affordable vacation available at that time, I have to say that camping became a wonderful blessing for me over the years. God can take limited finances—true for many pastors' families—and turn that into something wonderful.

Whenever we were in a national park, we always attended the worship services with our sons. One year my seven-year old son and I went to all our "neighbors" and invited everyone to a worship service at our campsite. Six or eight people from various church backgrounds joined us, and it was a special time. We read scriptures, shared a little, had a prayer time, and sang "Joy to the World" in the middle of July.

With deep sadness Howard and I recently gave up camping and sold our camper.

CHAPTER 7

VARIETY KEEPS
A PASTOR ON HIS TOES

EVERY PASTOR KNOWS that he will often receive odd requests.

My parents were active in a horseback-riding club that was actually a sheriff's posse on horseback for the men of my hometown. My dad was a very active member. This group had its own rodeo grounds on their property. On Sundays, they often had a worship service. One year, when Howard and I were visiting, he received an invitation to preach for that group. I've heard of pastors preaching at drive-in theaters, but Howard preached to about thirty horses and their riders that morning. It went something like this: "Snort." "Stamp." "Whoa!" "Steady, boy!"

He would probably tell you, though, that his most nightmarish memory involved another preaching engagement near our hometown. We were staying with my folks, but the church was in a small town about fifty miles away. Howard needed a haircut, and—wouldn't you know—my dad had a brand new haircutting kit! How my daddy came to fancy himself as a fine barber, I'll never know, because—well, I just wish I had a picture to show you what he did to Howard.

Howard sat on a stool in their den, and Daddy clipped away. I happened to walk into the room, and my unchecked response was, "Oh, Daddy!" To say Howard paled at that moment is an understatement.

Daddy, however, responded with, "What do you mean, 'Oh, Daddy?'" The resulting haircut looked exactly like Daddy had put a bowl on Howard's head and then peeled all of Howard's dark hair up to it.

The next day, Howard got up to preach on a chancel with a central pulpit, well aware that the choir behind him had a perfect view of my daddy's barbershop skills. The effect was quite colorful—the back of Howard's neck had a deep tan, then it was snowy white, topped off with Howard's black hair in a bowl shape. I observed several smiles coming from the choir as Howard led worship and preached.

But the strangest request for my pastor husband came late in his ministry. A young woman appeared at our door one day to ask Howard a favor. It was her mother's birthday, and the family was going out to eat later that day. This young woman wanted Howard to come to the restaurant to present her mother with the family gift: a brand new drainage hose for the toilet tank of their motor home! What can I say? Howard turned a few different colors then turned her down. There have to be some boundaries, right?

42

As we look back on that experience now, however, we both know it would have been a small matter to comply with her request, and thus to honor Jesus and her by doing so.

CHAPTER 8

CALIFORNIA DAYS

ONE OF OUR ministry moves led us to California. Howard was called from our Colorado congregation to be on a staff of a large church in Los Angeles. Although he knew it would be very hard to leave Colorado, he accepted the call.

We lived there only two-and-a-half years, but he gained valuable experience that served him well in his next pastorate. In fact, some of our most amazing experiences happened there.

The move out to LA found us with a car full of children, a dog, and a cat. Since we never traveled with a cat before, we assumed that we would stop on occasion to "walk the cat" in the same way we walked our dog.

The first afternoon of our trip, we stopped on a dirt side street in the small town of Montrose, Colorado (the very town we chose for our retirement home years later). Howard attached the leash to the big, beautiful Persian named Clyde and began to walk him. Clyde felt this experience was beneath his dignity and pulled back on the leash. What naturally followed, of course, was a tug of war.

Howard probably would have won, but we'll really never know because a farmer drove up in his pickup, rolled down the window and shouted to Howard, "He don't lead too well, do he?"

I cannot remember how Clyde made it the rest of the way to Los Angeles. I only know he was never on a leash again.

We came to own Clyde in a somewhat unusual way: he hung around the church one day too many. So our church organist called me and asked if we would like to have a cat. I did the unthinkable with such a request. I made a unilateral decision and said "yes."

Howard came home from church the next day (a Sunday) and did not immediately change out of his brand-new Arrow dress shirt. The doorbell rang and he and Beau Beagle went to the door together. When Howard opened the door, two things happened: The organist shoved Clyde into Howard's arms and dashed off, and Beau Beagle lunged for the cat, barking wildly. At that point, Clyde's claws found Howard's new shirt and shredded the front of it, drawing blood. It is astounding that even after that fiasco, Howard agreed to keep the cat.

When we moved to Los Angeles, we needed to purchase our own home. Various members of the congregation kindly offered their hospitality while we were house shopping. The first home we occupied belonged to a couple that Howard had married back in Colorado a few years before. They said we could stay there for three weeks. There was no backyard for our dog and cat, only a swimming pool surrounded by a walkway and some palm trees. Clyde was tethered to a palm tree.

We were quite comfortable in this home, though. After about five days, I noticed that whenever we were away, someone would run the dishwasher. Finally, the lady of the house called us and said they never actually left town. They were involved in a car accident. Not wanting to tell us, they had been spending the days at a relative's apartment. Unfortunately, her husband had injured his back in the accident, and he needed to be in his own bed. We were asked to move out.

The elder in charge of taking care of us called the next member he had lined up to host us. After a night in a motel, we drove to the lovely home and pulled into the driveway. The lady of the house met us at the car window, looked at who and what was in the car, and said without greeting us, "Oh, I wish I'd said 'no.'"

Then she proceeded to guide us to her pool house where we were to stay for the next week. The furnishings were two twin-sized beds. Remember, there were four of us! The kitchenette had no pots, pans, and worst of all, no coffee pot!

I stood in the middle of the kitchen and told Howard, "It will take a real act of grace to stay here for a week."

Whenever this woman had friends over to swim (she never invited us to use the pool, by the way), we had to vacate the pool house. I'm pleased to report, however, that grace abounded, and we made it the whole week. After that, we stayed in two other homes before closing on the one we bought. A little humility, pluck, and determination, underpinned by the marvelous grace of God, got us through that time.

At Christmas that year, we gave this woman and her physician husband a poinsettia. The next time I saw her, she expressed her amazement as she told me that no one had ever done anything like that for them. Ah, the mysterious ways God works to "gift" His children!

Los Angeles proved to be a great place for the boys and me, but not so great for Howard. However, he did a wonderful job with his staff duties. In the two-and-a-half years of our stay, several hundred people went through the new members class he designed. He also taught the single young adults how "loved, accepted, and forgiven" they were in Christ. While we were in that church, as an associate pastor's wife I was able to shed any stereotype I might have carried before. It was a wonderful, but brief time of just being me.

During this time, we were also on the Young Life Committee for a part of the San Fernando Valley. Since both boys were now in school, I had a chance to venture out into some of my own interests, so I took the Chaplain's Training Course at UCLA Medical Center. One woman in that group was the wife of a producer of the Billy Graham movies. She invited all of us to a premier of Graham's latest movie, and I gladly went, bringing with me two Jewish ladies who were in the class.

I'd be happy to tell you they were converted by this experience, but I really can't say if they were or not. I did enjoy their company, though. All in all, though our stay was brief, I believe the Los Angeles ministry opportunity gave me many chances for growth in my faith through an outstanding church and its leadership. I have always been grateful for the whole experience.

CHAPTER 9

FRIENDSHIPS GROW FROM CHURCH TO CHURCH

IN ALL OUR years of ministry, we have always carried one piece of luggage: wonderful, longtime friends. Thanks to computers, we correspond quickly and often with them. Some I haven't seen for over thirty years, but we write as if we never had time and distance between us.

Not long ago, Howard and I met for lunch in another town with two couples from the church in Colorado. We left there over thirty-five years ago. Sweet memories, a few tears, and loads of laughter were shared around that Mexican meal. The golden thread running through God's people is the strongest and most beautiful connection in the world. How grateful we are to be part of it!

It didn't take me long to figure out that every place in the Lower 48 where I had wanted to live, God had laid on the table for us. Now, that's pretty incredible, don't you think? It's true. Next up in pastorates was in the Pacific Northwest, a location I had never seen but had always wanted to visit. The timing was a little hard on me, though, because my aging parents were not in good health, and I really hoped to move more toward "home" in Texas.

The Pulpit Nominating Committee was extremely persistent in their wish for Howard to come. One woman on the committee kept telling us that Howard just "looked like" their next pastor, whatever that meant.

We combined a vacation camping trip with a visit to Yakima, Washington, to look it over. A lovely couple opened their home to us, our two boys, and (what else?) Beau Beagle. When we drove up, they immediately insisted that we bring our dog into the house. We, in turn, assured them that he was very well behaved and had been housebroken for years. That was all true—except at their house. When we went in, Beau Beagle went straight to their lovely wallpapered dining room wall and lifted his leg! You might think by now that I would hate beagles, but the truth is, I love them. I'll just never own another one.

When Howard said yes to the Yakima call, we loaded up our two cars with our two boys, two dogs, one cat, and a gerbil to drive thirteen hundred miles north. (Stay tuned: the next move included a goldfish.)

In Yakima, our youngest son was born. I was in my late thirties by then, and Howard was in his early forties. Our two older sons were eleven and eight-and-a-half. The word was that the church there had never had a pastor who had a newborn while he was there, so it was a pretty big deal to the congregation.

However, one woman had mixed feelings, I suppose. I met her one day in a downtown store, and she said, "I would have thought you were finished with your family." In a way, her comment typifies an underlying premise on which some members of congregations operate: that it's fine to say anything to a pastor and his family, no matter how rude or tactless. I have yet to figure out the psychology behind this, but each member of our family has scars to prove it. It was like *our* Christian faith, unlike theirs, was supposed to have some mysterious suit of armor around it that "sticks and stones and words" could never harm.

These were good opportunities to practice the same forgiveness I had received in Christ. Sometimes, however, I must confess I just carried the hurt and resentment instead. I was not always good at keeping short accounts or speaking up for myself in such instances.

I learned many fun things in Yakima, though I constantly struggled with feeling out of place. The older folks in our congregation were lovely people who had great values. Some of the younger women taught me canning. Yakima is right in the middle of fruit country—not just apples but pears, apricots, and plums. Our associate pastor's wife (now our son's mother-in-law) would go with me to a farm and pick chile peppers. I would take mine home and make a beautiful bright red ristra to hang in the kitchen.

Our sons helped me pick fruit when we visited the orchards. Even the little three-year-old would get in on the act. It was my first experience of living in an agricultural setting, and it was very rewarding. In the fall, my husband and I worked at the county fair in the Young Life booth making BBQ sandwiches. I loved the whole atmosphere. So did our sons.

Meanwhile, the tug to be in Texas was growing stronger. One spring, Howard, the two older boys, and I went to Young Life's Malibu Camp in Canada for a work week. Our only communication there was by radio. Shortly after we arrived, one of my sisters radioed, "If you want to see Daddy alive, you need to come now!"

That presented a very big problem, because Malibu is accessible only by a seven-hour boat ride or by seaplane. All the staff at the camp gathered around us and prayed. We made the tough decision to finish out the week, and Daddy pulled through. We were so grateful!

Although our neighborhood in Los Angeles was mostly Jewish, our area in Yakima was Catholic. We lived a block from the Catholic school, two blocks from the Catholic church, and about four blocks from the Catholic hospital. Both neighborhoods were truly gifts to our family. We had such great friends among those who lived around us. I met for prayer and sharing with two of my Catholic neighbors. Howard and I were often included in the family gatherings and special occasions of one family in particular.

When we left Los Angeles, one of my Jewish neighbors gave me an antique Episcopal prayer book for a going-away gift. I treasure any experience that broadens my understanding of God's all-encompassing love that reaches across, through, and above our self-imposed "religious" boundaries.

CHAPTER 10 ∾

GOD CALLS US BACK TO OUR ROOTS

SEVEN YEARS AFTER we came to Yakima, Howard was called to a church in our hometown, the same church where we were married in 1959. There are surprises, and then there are *surprises*!

This move would be another long one—from Yakima to Amarillo, Texas, and it had added dimensions. Again, we loaded up our two cars, but now we had three sons, Howard's mother, a dog, a cat, and a goldfish in a mayonnaise jar. It was around Thanksgiving time and frigid. We spent the first night on the road in Burley, Idaho. Sadly, when we unloaded the car at the motel the goldfish was overlooked, and the next morning, we found it frozen. Not a good way to start the day.

We were also moving into a manse again, after owning our own home in the past three locations. The manse was quite adequate, but it was next door to the church. Bordered on one side by the asphalt parking lot, the other side was next to a lovely park.

Living next door to the church had a unique effect on Howard. When he finally did get home, he was always looking at his office. He couldn't relax, knowing there was something or someone in that office needing his attention.

One of the stipulations of his call was that he would wait three years to call an associate. That's a long time for a pastor to be alone in a church of 600–800 members, give or take a lapsed member or two.

Previous trouble between the former senior pastor and an associate had caused this requirement. Meanwhile, high blood pressure and an ulcer let us know this wasn't working out well for Howard.

Ministering in our hometown had its own hardships. Local expectations seemed greater because folks remembered us from high school days. Friends from those years had no way of understanding the changes in us over the past twenty-two years, so we sometimes felt "in a box" from the past. We had lots of family there, and I really enjoyed our get-togethers for holidays and weddings. Sadly, there were funerals also. Howard was often called upon to perform a marriage ceremony of a family member or hold a funeral for another. This was not easy for him, but he kindly accepted.

My family members all belonged to other churches in Amarillo. Their perspective of the pastor's wife was based on what they experienced in their own congregations. Some of those wives were quite saintly and gracious. Some were hardly noticed. Some worked full-time outside the home. This caused some confusion in my family as they tried to fit me into some sort of stereotype, when they didn't know me well in my role as a pastor's wife.

One day, I went for a bike ride with my sister. We happened to meet up with her son's in-laws who were on a walk. This is how she introduced me: "This is my sister, Sondra. She's a minister's wife, but she's not like any other minister's wife you've ever known."

Like a deer in the forest, when I sense danger, I don't go there. So I never asked her why she introduced me that way. Another relative did not quite know what to do with our ministerial status. She usually introduced me to her friends by saying "This is Sondra. She's a minister's wife, so watch your language." This unfortunate comment usually created an awkward moment and made normal conversation very difficult.

I never worked out a script for dealing with that kind of situation. It was always a WWJD (What would Jesus do?) moment, but I did not have time to figure that out before they had hurried off to talk with someone else.

By the time we arrived in Amarillo, both my parents and Howard's mom were housebound and totally dependent on us. None of them drove. My sister and I worked together for our parents, sharing the duties, but she was still teaching school at the time.

Howard and I had two teenage sons, one kindergartner, three housebound parents, plus about 800 new souls to get acquainted with and minister to.

Every morning after our children went to school, I drove to my parents' house to fix their breakfast.

Meals-on-Wheels brought lunch, and my sister stopped on her way home from school to prepare their dinner. Meanwhile, Howard and I tried to help his mom a lot, too. By then, she was very frail and partially blind. This chapter in our life is not uncommon for many couples, whether in ministry or not. Somehow, we made it through as God provided the strength and help. When Howard and I managed to get away for a couple of days on our own, I remember that I often cried for the first fifty miles or so, inwardly, if not outwardly. It took me a full day to calm down and enjoy the trip.

While we were at this church I decided to take myself on a private retreat once in awhile. These were retreats either at the nearby Catholic Retreat Center or as far away as Ghost Ranch in New Mexico. I still gain strength by remembering how wonderful those experiences were. At Ghost Ranch I enjoyed brilliant, innumerable stars, an alfalfa field full of deer at dusk, walks alone among the sagebrush, or snow falling on cedars.

The following is an entry from one of my journals: "March 18, 1996: Arrived at Ghost Ranch for my 3-day R and R. There's a large group here for a writers' workshop, but it is still very quiet and tranquil. One of my greatest joys is listening to a classical station on the radio. I've heard everything from Fauré's *Requiem* to *West Side Story*.

March 19: The darkness of the night was awesome, literally, because of the brilliance and sheer numbers of the stars!" (I know this, because around 2:00 A.M., I went out and just stood for a while, looking up at the sky.) "Stayed in bed until 8:00 A.M., so I had breakfast in my room...accompanied by a classical concert, of course! Plans for the day: study, read, and walk (in any order I want!). Serendipities: the deer in the field, Vivaldi, reading John 16, walk toward Box Canyon, warm sun and cool breeze, so quiet. Tonight, new moon."

The Catholic Retreat Center had a fine library and bookstore, and I met Thomas Keating, Evelyn Underhill, and other great writers there. Sometimes I would read all night. I always returned home with joy and my spirit overflowing. It's hard for me to imagine what a pastor's wife might need more than a retreat where she sheds demanding duties for a few hours or days. One year I gave myself one for my birthday and spent that whole day in retreat.

I don't know if private retreats are common among other pastor's wives. I have yet to hear any of them share that they do that. A solo retreat does not replace large-gathering retreats, but it has a different purpose and different blessing. At least that is what I discovered when I took it up after many years in the pastorate.

Very shortly after Howard, our family, and I arrived in Amarillo, two couples who were not members came for a visit. They asked us if we would go over to the sanctuary with them and kneel on the steps to pray for the church. The six of us knelt there, and I remember how very much the prayers mentioned mission. The Lord was asked more than once to make that congregation a mission-minded church. I suppose I filed that away somewhere in my memory bank, because one day I looked up and realized their prayers had been answered.

Missions are very big in the life of that church. A young woman from the congregation went to Australia for a year (maybe two). Three young men went to Zaire to build a house near the hospital run by the Presbyterian Church. Eleven people went to Brazil to build a surgery unit in another mission hospital. Later on, another group from the church returned to that mission to work.

Every spring break finds a group doing mission work by building houses for Casas Por Cristo in Mexico, and in 1990 the church sent Howard and me to Zaire to encourage the pharmacist from our congregation in his mission work there. On that trip we brought ten footlockers brimming with medical supplies and gifts. Just recently I learned that nurses in this congregation have formed a group and have taken a mission trip to Nicaragua.

All congregations support missionaries, whether the missionaries are part of the congregation or not. The Amarillo church is unique because it sends out its own members to *do* mission work. We recently had a chance to tell the husband from one of those praying couples just how his prayers had been answered over the ensuing twenty-five years, and we're still counting.

CHAPTER 11

REFLECTIONS, REGRETS, AND REFRESHMENT

THE AMARILLO CHURCH was our last one before retirement, and we were there for seventeen years. When Howard retired in 1998, we moved to the Western Slope of Colorado. The adventures continue, and the beauty of this part of the world continues to bless us greatly. Last fall we moved to the Front Range to Fort Collins and are having new adventures, new grandchildren to visit, and meeting new people.

Recently, our sons treated me to a wonderful 70th birthday celebration, filled with awesome surprises. One son said to me, "You were a good pastor's wife all those years, Mom." My reply: "I don't know if I could do it again." And that's the truth.

But that is Sondra "in the flesh" speaking. My spirit tells me otherwise, because it all began in the mind of God in the first place. Remember, it's all about clay pots and the Master Potter, even though it sometimes feels more like being a goldfish in a mayonnaise jar—highly visible, yet overlooked or perhaps frozen out.

In retirement, new challenges have appeared. Like the one a wife wrote to me after her husband retired: "In these last few years I have realized that my identity has changed and sometimes I miss it. Although (her husband) seems satisfied to be out in the congregation, I sometimes miss having him in the pulpit." I certainly identify with that!

My heart has a special corner for all pastors' wives, and I pray for them. Once in awhile, in a gathering of pastors and wives or in some church setting, I hear the following comment from a pastor about his own wife or another pastor's wife, and my blood pressure always rises: "She keeps me in line." or "She keeps him in line."

What in the world does that mean, anyway? That sounds like someone referring to a lion-tamer. I find it insulting and trite when directed toward someone who deserves much more appreciation for the support she has been, the criticism and frustration she has dealt with, and the honor she has brought to the Lord.

I have never heard my own husband say that, by the way. In fact, he did just the opposite shortly before he retired. He wrote a tribute to me that was printed in our church newsletter. I was surprised, yes, but more than that—completely overwhelmed by such a loving gesture. Some wives in our congregation were waving that article in their husbands' faces. I know this, because they told me.

It is very important, however, that a pastor's wife not take herself too seriously. I had to learn that lesson over and over again. In our last church, I got a few more lessons.

In that church, one entered the sanctuary from the Christian Education area through a door next to the chancel. Thus, all those folks already seated in the pews could check out anyone coming in through that door. One Sunday I wore a favorite dress to church that I *thought* was dark navy blue. So I accessorized it with sheer navy hose and navy blue high heels. As I entered the sanctuary, I noticed a woman gazing hard at my outfit. *She must really like it,* I thought. Somewhere during the service, my eyes were opened, and I saw that my dress was, in fact, black.

Another Sunday, I entered the sanctuary from the parking lot, walked down the center aisle and took my seat on the aisle. Howard and his associate had already seated themselves on the chancel. As I looked up at them, I saw Howard get up and start directly toward me.

"How neat!" I thought. "He's coming to greet me." (Something he had never done so openly before a church service began.)

As I expectantly waited for him to greet me, he leaned over and said, "You have your sunglasses on." Silly guy. That's not a capital offense. One Sunday an associate pastor's wife wore her sunglasses during an entire church service to *protest* that the Father's Day picnic had been moved inside because of threatening rain. I wonder if the difference was that I was the *senior* pastor's wife?

Six Flags in Arlington, Texas, has a ride that lifts you 150 feet high on the outside of a tower. After a split-second pause, it drops you to the ground at breakneck speed. That may be an apt description of how these lessons always affected me. I could never be perfect in this life, no matter how hard I tried.

Identifying with the Apostle Peter comes easy for me—impetuous, at least one foot in his mouth most of the time, speaking up whether he had anything to say or not, "building booths" where they were not needed, missing the point of the teaching, sometimes rebuked by the Lord. Then, given another chance by Jesus, Peter reaffirmed his love and discipleship by saying, "Yes, Lord, you *know* that I love you" (John 21:17).

While holding Peter accountable, Jesus overlooked all the worldly warts of his personality and claimed him as His own forever. What could be better than that? Therein lies my hope and my joy…in a word, my *true* sense of self.

CHAPTER 12

JOY IN THE JOURNEY

A FEW YEARS ago I was asked to give a talk for the women's brunch that our church held around Christmastime. The theme was Love's Pure Light. When I received a call from a member of the Women's Ministry team asking me to be the speaker that year, I told her I would pray about it. I hung up the phone, had a short prayer with my husband, and called her right back to accept. Five minutes later she and another woman rang my doorbell.

They sat down in the living room, looked expectantly at me and asked, "What did God say to you?" I replied that it was the almost immediate, deep sense of peace I felt, and an assuring voice within that said, "You can do this."

I'll always, always be grateful for what God gave me to speak about that day: where does the Son of God, "Love's

Pure Light," meet us after Christmas, when all the tinsel is put away? The answer is "in His people." That is what I shared with the ladies. It's relevant in this book, as well, for pastors' wives who serve God's people.

Being a part of serving God's Church is a great privilege and honor. My husband and I have met thousands of God's people—Christ's followers and disciples—in our walk through the pastoral ministry. Many of them have been our reward and our joy and blessing, God's gifts to us.

Many have been saintly, generous, kind-hearted, pious in the best sense, humble, childlike, and yes, even eccentric in a fun way. Many have helped me grow in my faith as I observed their faith. I want now to introduce you to some of them who have been a part of our life and ministry, so you can meet these wonderful standouts in God's congregations.

I'll begin with Gracie Hendricks. She was a mentally-challenged eighteen-year-old with the learning abilities of maybe an eight-year-old. Gracie was in the youth group of the church we had in seminary. We lived in a town of only four hundred people, so everyone knew and accepted Gracie. It was no problem for her to be in our youth group. She came to our house on Saturdays to help a little by dusting or ironing Howard's handkerchiefs.

However, she did something else on those Saturdays, almost without fail. Howard would be upstairs working on his sermon, and Gracie would call out in her very distinctive voice, "Hey, Howard! Come look at this squirrel!" And you know what? We learned to go and stand beside her at the window every time she called out. Did you ever think squirrel-watching could be a Christ-like experience? Has there been a "Gracie" in your life?

Each of our three sons began reflecting the pure light of Christ to me when they were very small. Ben is our middle son. One Sunday evening I was driving the fifteen miles to church on an LA freeway with Sam, eight years old, and Ben, who was then six.

We were going back to church. I had a bad headache and an attitude to match. I wanted to be at home. After a few miles, I realized that Ben was singing as he sat beside me in the front seat. So I began to listen. He was singing "Amazing Grace" over and over, perfectly. After a bit of listening, I realized something else. My headache was gone! "Love's Pure Light" in the voice of a child.

My mother-in-law was a channel for the love and light of Jesus. She was widowed at the age of thirty-eight and had gone through many tough things. "Just tie another knot in the end of your rope," she would tell me, when things weren't going well. Her faith was simple, her trust rock-solid. She read her Bible the first thing every morning and the last thing every night.

I sometimes hear my husband tell someone, "I wish you'd known my mom. She was fun, and she was a great lady." Not educated beyond high school, not a women's leader in the church, just a steady, faithful, hard-working lady with lots of love to give. She sometimes slept through her son's sermons and always told him, "That was the best sermon I ever heard." He would catch her with, "Which part did you like best?" But she was ready for him as she replied, "Oh, I liked *all* of it!"

Dan was a homeless man who had an interesting lifestyle. He lived in his car, packed with everything he owned. He spent his days with his two school-aged children, driving from Oklahoma City to San Diego, then back—a very abnormal lifestyle, according to our social standards. Dan had developed a network of pastors on his route that provided the necessary meals, gasoline, beds, and showers to support his trips. We were in his network. He was a frustrating man in some ways. He wouldn't accept job offers. Yet, he was a gentle man of whom I was never afraid. I came to believe that Dan was more than a homeless wanderer. He was a Christian man.

One evening he sat at our piano and beautifully played and sang hymns for a long time, without any music. We always thought we were supposed to channel "Love's Pure Light" to him. I suspect it was the other way around. "Do not forget to entertain strangers, for by so doing some have unwittingly entertained angels." (Heb. 13:2 NKJV) Or the version I memorized long ago: "Do not neglect to show hospitality to strangers, for thereby some have entertained angels unawares." (RSV)

My friend and fellow church member, Melba, met the Lord in her late fifties. She was so grateful, she determined to serve Him with her whole heart, which she did. The Lord could send Melba to reflect His light in the darkest places. Melba had a ministry to prostitutes. I can't remember the details of how it began, but I do remember the day she met a man (the pimp, actually) in a parking lot on the boulevard and took two-year-old Justin from him.

Justin's mom was a druggie and a prostitute, and Melba convinced her that she could find a good home for him. Melba searched in the church carefully for a Christian couple to take Justin, but the longer it took (she was very careful in her search), the more she and her husband Frank grew to love him. Although both of them were up in years, Frank and Melba finally adopted Justin and undertook to raise him in the Lord.

Due to Justin's exposure to drugs in the womb, it was a very difficult task. Melba has done many things for the Lord, but this one thing has been a treasure to behold. Such a channel through which this pure light could shine! She would pray on the phone with our sons when they were sick, and she took our youngest son fishing in a nearby lake. She often left quiches on our doorstep with a note about the love of Jesus. An amazing servant was Melba.

All my Christian life I have sought Jesus in worship services and Bible studies, Sunday school and prayer meetings, in all the expected places. Yet I often found His light shining most brightly over a steam table, in a tollbooth, standing next to a custodial closet in a hospital, or on a playground. I still place myself in the expected settings and gain joy and strength for the journey there, but I want to be especially alert for the unexpected ones. I want to be like Melba.

CHAPTER 13

MONEY OR
THE LACK OF IT

I MENTIONED EARLIER that Howard's salary package in our first pastorate after seminary was $5,000. Recently we told our youth pastor this, and he replied, "Please tell me you are joking!"

Nope. That was it. In addition, we were paid once a month, so the "seventh-inning stretch" to make it to the end of the month was very difficult. When we adopted our first child, Howard went to Session and asked for twenty-five dollars more a month. A session member commented, "I don't know what you're doing with the money you already get."

So guess what Howard did? Before the next Session meeting, he made a list of where every penny of our earnings went. As he read the list to the members at the next session meeting, a lady elder asked, "Why are you doing this?" Why, indeed! How else would he have been able to justify his request for twenty-five dollars more? This experience was humiliating for him. It worked, though.

Sometime in our next pastorate, we began to use budget envelopes on a weekly basis, and we lived that way for many years after that. Another pastor's wife had told us about this method. We had an envelope for groceries, cleaning, entertainment, allowances, lunch money, clothing, and so forth. When the money was gone from the envelope, there was no more spending in that category until the next week.

Our three sons abided by that, too, although I did get a note on one occasion that read something like this: "Mom, I took ten dollars from the cleaning slot in the envelope, but I'm only spending five of it, which I earned yesterday mowing the lawn." This system really seemed to work and helped us to be disciplined in our spending.

I remember walking into a grocery store near the end of the month and praying, "Lord, I have exactly $12.00 to spend. Please help me shop wisely." The grocery bill was $11.99, and I didn't use a calculator while shopping! Experiences like this helped me to understand just how much God is in the details of our lives.

Eventually in our last pastorate before retirement, the envelopes were no longer necessary. Truthfully, we could never do anything extravagant, but at the same time, we never really lacked for the necessities of life or even a few luxuries once in awhile. Members of the congregation sometimes generously made their mountain cabins or second homes available to us for vacations. When it came time for college for our sons, monetary gifts from a church member donor would occasionally arrive to supplement their student loans.

When a new baby came into our family, there were baby showers, complete with new cribs or savings bonds. At Christmas, we were gifted in many ways—a package of steaks (what a treat!), a smoked turkey, homemade food items, gift certificates, toys, etc. One dear woman in Texas brought our Christmas breakfast every year for several years. She was a Home Economics teacher, and a marvelous cook. Such generous people we served all those years!

We managed somehow to buy the necessary bicycles, baseball mitts, and sneakers for three sons, send them to camp, buy school supplies and clothes, and pay for their prom dates. They found ways to earn their own money with newspaper routes, shoveling snow, mowing lawns, or working for some company or other when they became old enough. Student loans, scholarships, and jobs were available to help them get through college and one son through medical school (also supported by his working wife). Not a penny to spare, but enough to make it happen.

Howard and I were firm from the beginning about having a date night each week. After we had children, that practice became even more important. Somehow we managed to scrape together enough money for a sitter and a movie or a dinner out. Sometimes before we would go into the restaurant, we would sit in our car in the parking lot and "hash out" the stresses that had built up during the week. This was not so romantic, but necessary. Those times were more rare than normal, I'm glad to say.

When Howard was about to go to seminary, he received a three-year full scholarship that covered all his expenses. However, since he was pastor of a church during those years and took a lighter academic load, he had a fourth year to pay for. I worked full-time, and he received a small salary from the little church, so we began to save our money to pay for his fourth year in seminary. We had saved up about two hundred dollars when we got a call from a needy relative in another state. They needed exactly two hundred dollars for a house payment, or they would lose their home.

We sent them the whole amount. Meanwhile about this time, Howard's brother, a car salesman in another state, had taken our VW as a trade-in for a larger car. He sold the VW on his lot, and sent us the proceeds from his profit. We weren't expecting it, but he sent a check for two hundred dollars!

That is only one illustration, but the truth is, we've never, ever been able to out-give God. It's not just pastors and their families who have stories like this. God takes care of all His children in amazing ways, and I believe He really enjoys doing that. "And my God will supply every need of yours according to His riches in glory in Christ Jesus" (Phil. 4:19 RSV). Our part of the plan is to trust Him to do just that and then remember to say "thank you."

Probably one of the most helpful changes in our finances was when we began to receive housing allowances instead of living in manses. That way, we could purchase a home that fit our family and later sell it when we had to move. Every sale of a house resulted in a nice profit for us. That money often helped us buy furniture for the next home, if it was needed. I've always heard that the churches were better off, too, when they got out of the "housing" business.

Sometimes our house would not be sold before we had to move, so the new church would loan us a down payment for our next home. Then when we sold that house, we paid back the down payment. This actually worked out very well, and there were never any negative repercussions from this arrangement.

CHAPTER 14 ⌒

THE LAND OF UNLIKENESS

RECENTLY I RECEIVED a long e-mail from a pastor's wife we've known since seminary days. She and her husband are good friends and they are also retired now. I asked her to share from her story of their life in ministry. It paralleled our own story in many ways…the adventures, the hard lessons along the way, the hardship of some of the moves and how they affected the children, the occasional "backstabbing" by friends and members of the congregation, the criticism of one's pastor husband by those people, the differences in being an associate pastor's wife and being the senior pastor's wife, saying goodbye to good friends and relationships established in one parish as they moved to another.

They had a ministry experience, however, that was far different from others in our denomination: they served a congregation here in America that was mostly minorities. Over fifty languages were spoken in the local schools! Most of the people who lived in their condo building did not speak English.

Members of the pastor search committee left the church shortly after hiring her husband. A former pastor who was involved in an affair with one of the women elders, vented his anger by writing hateful notes to my friend's husband, accusing him of spying on this man's house.

All of these traumatic experiences took a toll on her husband's health. Yet, as she hurt for her husband, she continued to work hard in the church and made friends with some of the young couples. A blessing for her "sanity" came from her job at a local college, where she was appreciated and honored.

Finally, God did move them to the other side of the country to yet another uncommon ministry. As Auden said, "He is the way. Follow him through the land of unlikeness; you will see rare beasts, and have unique adventures."

Early in their marriage, as they left seminary and went west without a pastoral post, she commented that they did not worry. In her words, "We were on an adventure with God, and He would take care of us and He did." Later on, she closed her story with the following words: "I am thankful to God for these years, both the good and bad. He has always been faithful to us, and He has loved us through all our years." My hope is that her words are a resonating testimony for all pastors and their wives who have fought the good fight and run the race of their high calling in Christ Jesus.

Auden said it best:

"He is the life.
Love him in the World of the Flesh;
And at your marriage all its occasions shall dance
    for joy."

PW

LaVergne, TN USA
07 June 2010
185272LV00001B/6/P